Rethinking Baptism

Rethinking Baptism
Some Baptist Reflections

Stanley K. Fowler

WIPF & STOCK · Eugene, Oregon

RETHINKING BAPTISM
Some Baptist Reflections

Copyright © 2015 Stanley K. Fowler. All rights reserved. Except for brief quotations in critical publications or reviews, no part of this book may be reproduced in any manner without prior written permission from the publisher. Write: Permissions. Wipf and Stock Publishers, 199 W. 8th Ave., Suite 3, Eugene, OR 97401.

Wipf & Stock
An Imprint of Wipf and Stock Publishers
199 W. 8th Ave., Suite 3
Eugene, OR 97401

www.wipfandstock.com

ISBN 13: 978-1-4982-0967-0

Manufactured in the U.S.A.   08/17/2015

Contents

Preface | vii

Chapter 1: A Baptist Journey | 1
Chapter 2: A Look at the Biblical Texts | 11
Chapter 3: Questions and Answers | 32
Chapter 4: Conclusion | 56

Bibliography | 61

Preface

FOR THE LAST FEW months, I have been part of a national study team considering the possibility of a small change to the policy of my denomination about the relation between baptism and church membership. That experience has made me aware once again that tinkering with baptism among Baptists brings all sorts of strong feelings to the surface, but it also reminded me that Baptist emphasis on baptism tends to focus on the details of the human action, rather than what God might be doing in the event. In other words, Baptists are generally more certain about what does not happen in the sprinkling of an infant than they are about what does happen in the immersion of a confessing believer.

Anyone who takes seriously what we call the Great Commission (Matt 28:18–20) has to admit that baptism is about initiation into discipleship and thus very significant, but long ago I became convinced that my own tradition undervalued it. I tried to do something to change that when I wrote my doctoral thesis and later published it as *More Than a Symbol: The British Baptist Recovery of Baptismal Sacramentalism* (Paternoster, 2002). I am grateful that the book has been well received in many academic circles, but it has not become widely known at a more popular level, which comes as no great surprise. Some pastors who have found the book helpful have suggested that I write a shorter, more accessible book that focuses on the biblical evidence and practical applications. I thought about that occasionally, and I was finally prodded into action by Rick Reed, who became the president of our seminary in 2013.

Preface

I have written this book with pastors, aspiring pastors, and other church leaders in mind. While I hope it is rooted in solid scholarship, I have minimized the technicalities and attempted to write in a lucid and straightforward manner. The book has obvious relevance for Baptists, my own tribe, but also for many other denominational traditions that are credobaptist in practice. I think the book may also be interesting to paedobaptists, partly as a glimpse into the Baptist world, but also because all of us baptize confessing believers who have not been previously baptized, and there is value in taking a fresh look at our practice. Furthermore, in our post-Christendom society, many adults who want to become part of paedobaptist churches in the future will come as unbaptized persons.

Baptism is not the most important issue confronting the church today, but I am sure that it is designed by God to be an important part of Christian experience. If so, then there is value in rethinking our understanding and practice of baptism. Scripture is infallible, but our reading and application of Scripture are very fallible. I hope that this small book will in some way facilitate a fresh encounter with Scripture and reformation where necessary.

Chapter 1

A Baptist Journey

I LEARNED SOMETHING ABOUT the diversity of Baptist life early on, even though I was born to parents who were not yet believers. My maternal grandparents were Primitive Baptists, and my grandfather was a deacon in their church. I can still remember visiting that church occasionally, especially singing hymns from the shaped-note hymnal, and watching the members walk to the front to deposit their offering in the plate. My grandfather even made the wine for communion in his cellar at home. He was an abstainer, but primitivism demanded that the Lord's Supper be observed with the same fruit of the vine that Jesus used. Primitive Baptists have sometimes been called hardshell Baptists or anti-mission Baptists, because of their opposition to modern methods that they consider unbiblical. Their opposition to missionary societies is partly based on the absence of such agencies in the New Testament, and partly on their Hyper-Calvinistic theology. The term "Hyper-Calvinist" is often used loosely and unfairly to mean something like "more Calvinistic than I am," but in the case of the Primitive Baptists, it is a legitimate descriptor. On principle, they did not affirm a universal offer of the gospel, leaving all the work of calling sinners to Christ with God himself. However, in spite of this essentially fatalistic attitude, my grandfather was fervent in prayer. When I was three years old, suffering with viral pneumonia and appendicitis simultaneously, offered no hope by doctors, my grandfather prayed for days, and I lived to tell the story. Later, when I was a pastor, he prayed for me every Sunday at just the right time of day. We can be grateful that sometimes our practice is better than our theology.

Primitive Baptists were also opposed to theological schools on principle, but Oakland City, Indiana (where my grandparents' church was located) was also home to Oakland City College (now University), a General Baptist school. The General Baptists are Arminian in their theological commitments, that is, at the opposite end of the spectrum from the Primitive Baptists. We had neighbors who were committed disciples of Christ and members of the New Liberty General Baptist Church, and whenever my parents went to church, it tended to be there. One of my mother's cousins was also a student at Oakland City College, and on a couple of occasions I sat in on his classes. As a boy I had no understanding of the Calvinist-Arminian debate, but I was aware that there were at least two kinds of Baptists who didn't always appreciate each other. I don't know whether that division was a major factor, but for some reason my parents did not become believers at that point in my life.

My parents' conversion occurred when I was eleven years old, after relocating to the Indianapolis area. It was through the witness of longtime friends and in a revival meeting in a Baptist Church, but it was Regular Baptist and neither Primitive nor General. I later confessed my faith in baptism when I was thirteen years old in that church context, and I was a member there until I finished university and went away to seminary. One of the emphases of the Regular Baptist church was doctrinal purity and separation from apostates, which meant that I frequently heard attacks on the false doctrine of other kinds of churches. I don't recall that the unity of the wider church was ever a preaching theme. I will never forget the sermon that referred to the "backward collar Whiskeypalians," thus dealing with clericalism and drinkers in one neat phrase. Pastors in our circles were fond of dismissing others by labeling them, and it was crucial that we identify ourselves as "fundamentalists" instead of "neo-evangelicals." I think we admitted that there were other churches that affirmed much that was true, but we were committed to truth in its fullness. Perhaps I'm overstating it, but we were clearly very good at criticizing other kinds of "Christians."

Some of our strongest criticisms were directed at the churches in what is often called the Stone-Campbell tradition, sometimes at the Christian Church-Disciples of Christ (the ecumenically-oriented stream), but more often at the a cappella Churches of Christ (the most exclusive stream). There were various points of tension, but clearly the most significant was baptismal theology. The Churches of Christ were often called Campbellites, because of Alexander Campbell, the preacher who led the movement in the 19th century, and this division over baptism goes back to battles in that century between Campbell and the Baptists.

The heart of the debate is whether we get baptized to testify to a previously completed conversion experience (Baptists) or to experience the remission of sins (Churches of Christ). Do I come to baptism as a confirmed believer (Baptists) or as a repentant sinner turning to Christ (Churches of Christ)? Do I get baptized because I have been saved (Baptists) or in order to be saved (Churches of Christ)? Must I have a conversion narrative to tell prior to baptism (Baptists), or is confession of faith in Jesus Christ adequate (Churches of Christ)? The debate can be phrased in various ways, but it deals with the most fundamental realities of Christian experience, and therefore, it is an emotionally charged debate. In my experience at that point, there was little contact between the two camps—we talked about each other rather than to each other. I can still remember my pastor's assertion that we believed in the "power of the blood," but they believed in the "power of the tub." The idea that baptism was instrumental in the experience of salvation was condemned as works-righteousness and a false gospel, and my sense was that members of the local Church of Christ were not to be considered brothers and sisters in the faith. Of course, the same attitude prevailed on the other side of the divide. They did not think of us as brothers and sisters, because we had not been baptized intentionally "for the remission of sins" (in accord with Acts 2:38).

Rethinking Baptism

I had limited exposure to Church of Christ people while I was in high school, but my horizons expanded when I was in university. In order to save money on room and board in my third year in university, I lived in a co-op house sponsored by a local Church of Christ, and this created lots of opportunity to discuss doctrinal questions. After all this, I was still convinced that the typical Church of Christ perspective gave to baptism a power far beyond what could be correlated with justification by grace alone and through faith alone. In particular, the idea that baptismal confusion was a basis for condemnation seemed to view baptism in a semi-magical, unbiblical way, and to ground acceptance with God in clear thinking more than grace. But at the same time, I had to admit that there were several baptism texts in the New Testament that seemed to say that baptism was instrumental in salvation, and I found myself somewhat discontent with the standard Baptist rhetoric. I wondered if there might be a better way to say it, a way to synthesize the biblical witness that was somewhere between the two perspectives that I knew. I wasn't sure how to say it, but I had the growing conviction that there must be a better way.

While doing my degree in mathematics at Purdue University, I became convinced that God had equipped (and thus called) me to the ministry of the Word, and after university I went to Dallas Seminary to prepare for ministry. Although study at Dallas was a wonderful experience in many ways, it wasn't really a great help in thinking about baptismal theology. For many reasons, rooted in its non-denominational and dispensationalist ethos, the seminary sometimes seemed to be anti-denominational and uninterested in the ecclesiological issues that divided the various Christian traditions. I remember the day in class when the president of the school told us that in his opinion the New Testament gave almost no importance at all to water-baptism, focusing instead on the reality of Spirit-baptism. Occasionally, I would even hear the language of real (Spirit) baptism versus ritual (water) baptism. For obvious reasons, my thinking about baptism did not develop much while I was in seminary.

My first pastoral ministry was at Emmanuel Baptist Church in Bloomington, Indiana, and in that context I had to think more deeply about baptism in order to teach the doctrine, to explain it to baptismal candidates, and to articulate at baptisms what was going on in the event. During those years I became acquainted with G. R. Beasley-Murray's *Baptism in the New Testament*, which had been published about a decade earlier. Here was a book commended by scholars across the denominational spectrum, written by a British Baptist, treating every baptismal text and allusion in the New Testament in detail, and then synthesizing all of that into a theology of baptism in a way that I found utterly compelling. The book is still in print and is still considered by many to be *the* book on baptism. I suppose this was the first time I had ever encountered a Baptist who insisted that baptism is a "sacrament," a means of grace that in some sense conveys what it signifies.

Thinking through the argument of Beasley-Murray's book helped me to clarify my own thinking about baptism and to articulate a way of thinking about it that enabled a natural reading of biblical texts about baptism, while also avoiding what I took to be the overstatements of my Church of Christ friends. I found in the British Baptist tradition language about baptism that resonated with my developing understanding, although I had never heard it in my American context. I can't say that this new perspective radically transformed my pastoral practice, but it did force me to speak of baptism as an integral part of conversion. If I invited people to respond publically to the gospel, I began phrasing it in terms of commitment to baptism as the normal way to say yes to the gospel.

After five years in Bloomington, I accepted a call to become the Pastor of Runnymede Baptist Church in Toronto, Ontario. The reasons for that move constitute another long story, but one of the effects was that after two years in Toronto, I began teaching theology part-time at Central Baptist Seminary, fulfilling a sense of vocation that had long been present in me. That gave me the opportunity, indeed the necessity, to develop my thinking about baptism more extensively in order to teach aspiring pastors how to think about it. In the process, I became more convinced than ever that baptism in biblical terms is conversion-baptism, and thus a meeting-place of grace and faith, the sacramental seal of the experience of union with Christ. I recognized, of course, that such language was atypical in my circles, and I knew that I had to use such language carefully. Certainly terminology was not, and is not, the basic issue. Whether we call baptism a "sacrament" or an "ordinance," we have to explain what we mean by the term. Neither term is an explicitly biblical way to describe the category that includes baptism and the Lord's Supper, nor are the terms mutually exclusive. My growing concern was to recover the sense of baptism as an initiation into Christian experience, rather than a witness to previous Christian experience.

After teaching theology part-time in addition to pastoral ministry for a few years, I became convinced that I needed to purse a research doctorate in theology and move toward full-time academic work. I was accepted into the doctoral program at Wycliffe College at the University of Toronto, so I resigned from my pastoral ministry and began studies there in 1985. Wycliffe is an evangelical Anglican school that is part of the Toronto School of Theology, a consortium of four Protestant and three Roman Catholic seminaries on the university campus. My course work there allowed me to get first-hand exposure to many streams of Christian thought, including the diverse theologies of baptism. In my first semester of courses, I did one on baptism in the early church with a Jesuit scholar; later I did a course focused on Volume IV/4 of Karl Barth's *Church Dogmatics*, much of which represents Barth's final statement on baptism; and I did an independent reading course on post-World War II baptismal theology under the direction of John Webster at Wycliffe.

As I was thinking about a topic for my doctoral thesis, I kept coming back to my interest in baptismal theology, and I discussed my thinking with John Webster, the theologian at Wycliffe who would likely serve as my thesis director. By that time I had become aware that the work of Beasley-Murray was actually the culmination of fresh thinking about baptism that had been going on for decades among British Baptists. As a result I suggested to John that I might do a theological analysis of that twentieth-century reformulation, and he thought that the idea had merit. He suggested that I start by investigating the earlier British Baptist literature on the meaning of baptism, in order to understand the historical background. When I began reading the foundational Baptist literature of the seventeenth century, I was pleasantly surprised to find that the early Baptists often spoke of baptism in the ways that I had come to appreciate, freely describing it in sacramental terms and sounding more like Church of Christ theologians than the Baptists around me. When I wrote a preliminary analysis of that early Baptist literature and gave it to John, he told me that I might reorient Baptist studies if I proceeded with the thesis, and he encouraged me to proceed, but carefully, because he didn't want me to lose my job over it! I'm thankful that to this point, what he envisioned has not occurred (at least the job loss).

I began reading widely in Baptist literature on the meaning of baptism around 1988, in order to create a viable thesis proposal that would analyze the twentieth-century British reformulation historically, biblically, and theologically. In a way that I had never planned, I was drawn into academic administration at Central Baptist Seminary in a time of crisis, which resulted in facilitating a merger with London Baptist Bible College and Seminary in 1993 to create Heritage College & Seminary. It was important work that had to be done, but it left virtually no time to advance the thesis research. Ultimately I was granted a twelve-month study leave in 1996–1997 to return to the doctoral program and write the thesis. That gave me the chance to immerse myself in the literature and to ultimately do the oral defense of the thesis in May 1998. I had now declared myself in print and had become a public advocate of Baptist sacramentalism.

Most scholars who complete a doctoral thesis would like to get it published, and I was no exception, but I wasn't quite sure where to start. When I had been nearing the end of a first draft of my thesis, I learned of a similar thesis that had just been submitted by Anthony Cross at the University of Keele in England. Fearing that mine might now be redundant, I immediately got in touch with Anthony, but I discovered that his was a broad history of theology and practice among British Baptists in the twentieth century, while mine was a focused analysis of the theology. His thesis was published as *Baptism and the Baptists* by Paternoster Press in 2000, and later that same year Anthony and I met at the second International Conference on Baptist Studies in North Carolina. By that time he was doing part-time editorial work for Paternoster, and he encouraged me to submit my thesis for possible publication. Thanks to Anthony's support, my work was accepted for publication. It was originally to be one volume in the Paternoster Biblical and Theological Monographs, the academic segment of Paternoster's publications. However, by the time my book was to be published in 2002, Paternoster had decided to launch a series called "Studies in Baptist History and Thought," and my book thus became Volume 2 in that series, *More Than a Symbol: The British Baptist Recovery of Baptismal Sacramentalism*.

My book has been well received by Baptists in various parts of the world and is frequently referenced in later works on baptism, but it has not been as widely read or easily accepted in North America. Shortly after its publication in 2002, I was at a meeting of Baptist historians and theologians in Kansas City, and I was showing a copy of the book to two friends there. One of the men, who essentially shared my view, said that when he teaches the topic in his Baptist school, on the first day the students think he is a heretic, but by the second day they are more receptive. My other friend indicated that he was having a hard time getting to day two. Ten years later, I was talking to this second friend at another conference, and he still has difficulty accepting my conclusions.

One of the difficulties in this discussion is the term "sacramental," given the diverse ways in which the term is defined in the various Christian traditions. The term as applied to baptism indicates that baptism is in some sense a means of grace, an effective sign that conveys in some sense what it signifies. But the challenge lies in defining that "sense" in which it is instrumental in conveying the benefits that it signifies. The Roman Catholic idea of sacrament is not equivalent to the Lutheran idea, or the Reformed idea, or the Stone-Campbell idea, or the Baptist idea. One of the best books on baptism in recent years is *Believer's Baptism: Sign of the New Covenant in Christ*, edited by Thomas Schreiner and Shawn Wright and published by an agency of the Southern Baptist Convention. Several chapters in the book, including the one on the New Testament epistles by Schreiner, interpret baptism in basically the same way that I do (at least in my opinion), but in a footnote in the editors' introduction, they indicate their reluctance to admit that my book runs along the same track as theirs, largely because I am willing to adopt sacramental terminology.[1] Other Baptist writers give evidence of affirming that baptism is more than a retrospective symbol, that it is in fact instrumental in some way in becoming a Christian, but they tend to be wary of sacramental language.[2]

Schreiner and Wright struggle to accept my proposal, but a full-scale Baptist attack can be found in David Gay's *Baptist Sacramentalism: A Warning to Baptists*. The author is an English Baptist, and his attitude should be obvious from the title. He is concerned about the wider emphasis on sacramentalism among British Baptists, but my book serves as an opponent throughout the book. He seems to be convinced that people like me are headed inevitably down the road to paedobaptism (the baptism of infants) and ultimately to Roman Catholicism. I understand the concern, even though I believe that his critique is overstated. As I have stated above, my concern is not about terminology, but is in fact about letting the baptism texts of the New Testament speak naturally, and with that in view to test the adequacy of typical Baptist ways of stating the meaning of baptism.

It is ironic that Baptists, in spite of their name, often minimize baptism in practice. For them, conversion is typically thought of as complete prior to baptism, so that baptism is reduced to sheer obedience, often as nothing more than a final hoop to jump through

---

1. Schreiner and Wright, *Believer's Baptism*, 2.
2. A brief description of this evidence can be found in Fowler, "Baptists and Churches of Christ in Search of a Common Theology of Baptism," in *Baptist Sacramentalism 2*, 254-269.

for church membership. But in spite of this low view of baptism's efficacy and an insistence that it is purely symbolic of something past, it is still required as a condition of church membership even for those who were baptized in infancy and have been living as disciples of Jesus for decades. I agree that baptism, as a confessing believer, should be required for church membership, but this is much more intelligible if baptism is more than a symbol.

Given the traditional Baptist emphasis on the unique and final authority of Scripture, we should be prepared to take a fresh look at the biblical witness to baptism and ask whether our ideas about baptism are an adequate way to describe that witness. That may be radical, but surely it is right.

Chapter 2

A Look at the Biblical Texts

I HAVE HAD SOME memorable experiences baptizing people, but one of the most memorable baptismal experiences occurred when I was just an observer. It was during my first pastoral ministry, at Emmanuel Baptist Church in Bloomington, Indiana. I was observing, because a small congregation in town with no baptistery in their building had borrowed our building for the afternoon. When the first candidate for baptism had entered the tank, the pastor read from Peter's words to the crowd at Pentecost, "Repent and be baptized, every one of you, in the name of Jesus Christ for the forgiveness of your sins (Acts 2:38)." He then turned to the woman about to be baptized and said, "Now, do you understand that your baptism has absolutely nothing to do with your personal salvation?" The idea expressed came as no surprise to me—I had heard the same thing in various forms many times—but I could hardly imagine reading Acts 2:38 in preparation for the comment. It would make more sense to forbid the reading of that text in that situation.

What happened that day in the baptismal tank, however, is a particularly vivid illustration of the difficulty that most Baptists and many other evangelical Christians have in teaching baptismal doctrine from baptismal texts. What often happens is that we develop a doctrine of conversion and salvation from a select group of texts in the Pauline epistles. These texts emphasize the "faith alone, grace alone" nature of salvation, and then the baptismal texts are forced onto that grid on the assumption that "faith alone" means "by faith and not by baptism." But it seems to require some interpretive gymnastics to make the baptism texts of the New Testament fit that grid, with Acts 2:38 being only one of the most obvious examples. Now, what would happen if we tried to develop a baptismal theology based on the actual baptism texts? Although that seems like an obvious approach to take, it is often not done. Rather than speculating as to why that is so, I propose to survey the explicit NT references to baptism and some of the apparent allusions, and on the basis of those texts to formulate a way of thinking about the relation between baptism and the salvation that it signifies.

The Baptism of John (Matthew 3:1–12; Mark 1:4–8; Luke 3:1–18; John 1:19–34)

There is no simple equivalence between the baptism of John and Christian baptism, but it is hard to deny that there is overlap between the two, especially in view of the fact that Jesus' disciples were baptizing at the same time as John (John 4:1–2). Although the benefits signified by the two baptisms are anticipatory for John, and in some sense fulfilled after Pentecost, there would seem to be similarity in the way each baptism relates to the things signified by it; in particular, in each case there is some sense in which the sign leads to the things signified.

Both Mark and Luke indicate that John's is a "baptism of repentance for the forgiveness of sins" (Mark 1:4; Luke 1:3). Although the ultimately crucial thing is clearly the attitude of repentance and its fruits, the act of baptism is the vehicle of repentance and thus a means of experiencing the forgiveness of sins. It is not that one repents, experiences forgiveness, and then is later baptized, but rather that the attitude of repentance comes to tangible expression in the act of baptism. Matthew does not use exactly the same words, but he does indicate that baptism is the act in which sins are confessed (Matt 3:6), which is to say that baptism looks forward to forgiveness. Matthew also records Jesus' words recognizing that those who are coming to be baptized are doing so in order to escape the eschatological wrath of the day of the Lord (3:7). In other words, John's baptism is described as a divinely provided means to be forgiven for one's sins in anticipation of the coming of the kingdom of God, a means by which one escapes the wrath of that day and enters the kingdom. The act has no power in itself, of course—this is not about ritual magic. That is made clear in Jesus' rebuke of insincere Pharisees and Sadducees who were submitting to the ritual but without any felt need for anything beyond their connection to Abraham (Matt 3:7–9; Luke 3:7). The power is not in the ritual of baptism, but baptism is done as a way of experiencing the salvation of the kingdom of God through repentance.

All of the Gospels record John's promise that the Messiah who comes after him will baptize in the Holy Spirit (Matt 3:11; Mark 1:8; Luke 3:16; John 1:33), as opposed to John's baptism that is merely in water. The baptismal language in reference to Jesus' future work could be a purely metaphorical description of the gift of the Spirit to new covenant believers, or it could be a suggestion that the coming baptism in the Spirit will be connected to baptism in water in the name of Jesus. We will need to look at the way in which the rest of the New Testament treats those subjects to answer that question.

Matthew 28:18–20

Aside from the passing reference in John 4, nothing is said about the baptizing activity of the apostles during Jesus' earthly ministry, but baptism figures prominently in the parting words of the Lord prior to his ascension. His words as recorded by Matthew are often called the Great Commission, but many explanations of his words make baptism something like the "great omission," or at least a mere afterthought. Baptists have often read and taught the text this way: "Go and make disciples of all nations, then after they have become disciples by faith, baptize the disciples and teach them to obey my commands."[1] John Gill argued that the object of "baptizing" here must be disciples and not the nations, because the Greek word for "them" is *autous*, which is masculine in gender, while the word for "nations" (*ethnē*) is neuter in gender.[2] Read this way, the baptizing activity follows the disciple-making activity, and this has the benefit of supporting the restriction of baptism to those who have already confessed faith in Christ (as opposed to the baptism of believers' children). This reading of the text also lends support to the typical Baptist assumption that new believers must prove the reality of their conversion prior to baptism, which then functions as a backward-looking witness to a completed conversion.

This typical Baptist reading of the text is simply not convincing. As has been pointed out by many contemporary teachers, there is grammatically one imperative in the text (make disciples), one aorist participle (having gone, go), and two present participles (baptizing, teaching). An aorist participle normally denotes action that is logically (if not temporally) prior to the action of the main verb,[3] leading to a translation like "Having gone, make disciples" or "Go and make disciples." Matthew's use of this Greek word (*poreuthentes*) in this construction elsewhere (2:8; 9:13; 11:4; 17:27; 18:12; 22:15; 26:14) suggests that the participle essentially takes on the imperatival nuances of the main verb, and this supports the translation, "Go and make disciples." On the other hand, a present participle in Greek normally denotes action that occurs simultaneously with the main verb of the sentence,[4] and that implies that baptizing and teaching are not done after making disciples, but instead are done at the same time as making disciples. Baptizing and teaching are, therefore, the means by which disciples are made or the manner in which they are made. In other words, one becomes a disciple by baptism and grows as a disciple by ongoing obedience to Christ's commands.

1. For example, Gill, *Body of Divinity*, 901.
2. Ibid.
3. Mounce, *Basics of Biblical Greek*, 268.
4. Ibid., 255.

A Look at the Biblical Texts

The assertion by Gill and others that the shift from the neuter *ethnē* to the masculine *autous* means that the object of "baptizing" must be "disciples" rather than "nations" is also unconvincing. The same verbal shift occurs in Matthew 25:32, where we read that at the coming of Christ in glory all the nations (*ethnē*) will be gathered before him, and he will separate them (*autous*) into two groups with two eternal destinies. Clearly the two words denote the same people in that text, with the first word describing humans as people groups, and the second as individuals. Similarly in Matthew 28:19, the use of *autous* is appropriate, because baptism is done to individuals and not to nations as groups, but this does not imply that the individuals baptized are already disciples prior to their baptism.

This text also describes baptism as a means by which we are brought into connection with the Triune God. The words of Jesus are typically translated "in the name of . . . " and the phrase is routinely spoken in the act of baptism—for some, the validity of the baptism depends on the liturgical phrase. However, we need to note that the Greek preposition used in the phrase is not *en* but *eis*, a preposition that commonly conveys directional nuances and thus is often rendered "into." The word is often used with the verb *pisteuō* ("believe") to indicate that faith in Christ is about attachment to or commitment to Christ. So we might appropriately translate Jesus' words as "baptizing them *into* the name of the Father, and the Son, and the Holy Spirit." In biblical usage, "the name" of God is really another way of denoting God himself, so that "baptizing into the name" of God is equivalent to "baptizing into God", i.e., baptizing into communion/fellowship with God. Baptism is Trinitarian in nature, because in it we experience reconciliation with the Father through faith in the Son, having been drawn to faith by the Holy Spirit (who is also bestowed on us by the risen Son as a benefit of the new covenant). All this is further evidence that the words of Jesus describe baptism as a means by which we enter into communion with God, not as a mere symbol pointing to a prior reality.

Acts 2:38

At Pentecost God poured out the Holy Spirit through the risen Christ, in fulfillment of his promise through the prophets (e.g., Joel 2) and John the Baptist, marking this major transition with powerful signs. In Peter's proclamation explaining all of this, he tells Jews who rejected Jesus the Messiah that God has vindicated him as the Lord who is now exalted in heaven but will return to crush his enemies (2:35–36). As the Spirit drove home this truth to the listeners, they asked what they could do to avoid the wrath of the risen Messiah-King-Judge (2:37), and Peter's answer was clear: they should repent and be baptized in the name of Jesus (2:38). The divine response would include both the forgiveness of their sins and the gift of the Spirit who had just been poured out. The words are "repent and let each one of you be baptized . . . " with the plural command to repent being addressed to the entire crowd, all of whom could change their mind simultaneously, and the singular command to be baptized being addressed to them individually, as they would each in turn express their repentance in the ritual act. Baptism is clearly an integral part of the conversion demanded, sufficiently so that Luke's description of their response is in terms of their baptism, not explicitly in terms of their repentance (2:41).

This text seems to say quite clearly that baptism is done as a means of experiencing the benefits of saving union with Christ, but that is not easily affirmed by the many Baptists (and others) who see a threat to salvation by faith alone, apart from works. As a result, Baptists have often been inclined to follow the lead of their most famous Greek scholar, the late A. T. Robertson of Southern Baptist Theological Seminary. Robertson argues that the preposition *eis* sometimes has a causal meaning, and that this verse should be translated "because of the forgiveness of sins," i.e., because of forgiveness already experienced via repentance prior to baptism. He writes:

> One will decide the use here according as he believes that baptism is essential to the remission of sins or not. My view is decidedly against the idea that Peter, Paul, or any

A Look at the Biblical Texts

one in the New Testament taught baptism as essential to the remission of sins or the means of securing such remission. So I understand Peter to be urging baptism on each of them who had already turned (repented) and for it to be done in the name of Jesus Christ on the basis of the forgiveness of sins which they had already received.[5]

There is no doubt about Robertson's ability as a Greek scholar, but there are many reasons to reject his interpretation of this passage. First, the very existence of the causal sense of *eis* is a disputed point among Greek scholars.[6] Second, and more to the point, the wider use of *eis* with "forgiveness of sins" as its object consistently shows forgiveness to be the result of *eis*, not the condition of *eis*. Matthew 26:28 describes the forgiveness of sins as the result of the pouring out of the blood of Christ. Luke 24:47 (in some manuscripts) envisions the forgiveness of sins as the result of preaching the gospel to all nations. Both Mark 1:4 and Luke 3:3 describe John's baptism as a request for forgiveness of the sins confessed in baptism. It is, then, natural to read Acts 2:38 as a statement that forgiveness is sought by baptism.

Robertson's statement of his view makes it clear that his conclusion is determined by prior theological commitments, not by the natural sense of the Greek words in the text. He clearly assumes that if *eis* denotes purpose (not cause) here, then there can be no salvation apart from baptism, but this is an unfortunate misreading of the language. Peter is not addressing the possibility of salvation for those who might genuinely repent but for some reason be unbaptized—he is describing the way in which God designed baptism to function with no intent to say that God's grace is bound by baptism. Robertson's concern to avoid a magical or mechanical view of baptism is appropriate, but the answer can be found within Acts itself (notably in chapter 10, see below) without resorting to forced exegesis.

---

5. Robertson, *Word Pictures*, 3:35–36.

6. The causal use is defended by Mantey, "The Causal Use of *eis* in the New Testament," 45–48, but countered by Turner and Moulton, *A Grammar of New Testament Greek*, 3:266.

Acts 8

At this point in the narrative of Acts, Luke records the progress of the gospel beyond Judea into Samaria, and baptism is a prominent feature in the description of response to the gospel. Philip proclaimed the message about Jesus the Messiah there (8:5) and supported his verbal communication by performing exorcisms and miraculous healings (8:6–7). When the Samaritans believed the message about Jesus the Messianic King, their response was to be baptized (8:12). Luke indicates that among those who believed and were baptized was Simon, a sorcerer who had captivated the Samaritans with his supernatural activity (8:9–11, 13). For reasons not specified in the narrative, the Holy Spirit was not poured out immediately on these new believers, but instead was conveyed later through the prayer of the apostles Peter and John, who were sent from Jerusalem to investigate (8:14–17).

The significance of baptism as a defining moment in conversion can be seen here in at least two ways. First, Luke's description of those who responded positively to the gospel is given in terms of baptism. Their response is not described in terms of a prayer or some other way to translate belief into action, but in terms of their being baptized (8:12). And when the temporal gap between conversion and the gift of the Spirit is described, Luke does not say that "they had only believed," but rather that "they had simply been baptized in the name of the Lord Jesus (8:16)." The converted are the baptized—there is no distinction between the two. Second, the place of Simon in the narrative shows us that baptism occurs at the initial profession of faith, not at some later point after demonstrating the genuineness of one's profession. We aren't told in the narrative how much time expired between the Samaritans' baptisms and the coming of the Spirit, but it was clearly only as long as it took for news to travel to Jerusalem and for Peter and John to get to Samaria. If Philip thought that conversion should be proved prior to baptism, then he would surely have delayed Simon's baptism for that time period, given the prior reputation of the sorcerer. Ultimately, after the bestowal of the Spirit with evidential signs, Simon demonstrated through his crass request to buy apostolic power that his profession of faith was far from genuine (8:18–23), even though he had been described as believing and being baptized. Baptists today often worry about baptizing people who may not be truly saved, but there is no indication that Philip shared that anxiety. The evidence here indicates that nothing more than a credible profession of faith is required for baptism. The fact that some who have been baptized later fall away is not a basis for criticizing the baptizer, which ought to be clear to anyone who has pondered our Lord's parable of the sower.

The chapter continues with the account of Philip being directed by an angel to travel past Jerusalem on the road toward Gaza, where he met up with the treasurer of Ethiopia, who was returning home after worshiping in Jerusalem. Their conversation starts at Isaiah 53, and Philip explains that the prophetic anticipation found fulfillment in Jesus. The man is clearly prepared to believe whatever the prophet is saying, and recognizes the truth in what Philip is saying, and he perceives that the right way to affirm this truth is to be baptized (8:36). We are not told in the narrative how he learned about baptism and its function, but if he had spent much time in Jerusalem, it would be likely that he heard conversations about it there. Perhaps he went to Jerusalem at least annually; if so, he would no doubt have become familiar with the practice. In any case, he recognizes that the right way to respond to the message about Jesus is to be baptized, and he asks that Philip baptize him. Verse 37 (Philip's statement that the man may be baptized if he believes "that Jesus Christ is the Son of God") is almost certainly not part of the original text of Acts, as modern versions recognize, although the narrative of Acts up to this point consistently displays the connection between faith and baptism. We don't know what Philip said to the Ethiopian, but what we do know is that he baptized him at his request as a formal way to embrace the gospel and did not ask for evidence in any ongoing way. Whether in Samaria or Gaza, the believers and the baptized are the same people.

Acts 10

Peter's visit to the house of Cornelius is clearly a major turning point in Acts, in that it represents the first giant step toward Gentile inclusion in the covenant people. While Peter was explaining the gospel and offering forgiveness of sins to all who believe in Jesus (10:43), prior to any outward response on the part of the listeners, God poured out the Holy Spirit on the whole household (10:44) and signified it (as at Pentecost) by speaking in tongues (10:46). God thus altered the patterns seen earlier in the book and manifestly bestowed the Spirit apart from any ritual acts. At first glance, this might seem to abrogate the connection to baptism described earlier by Luke, but that would be a premature judgment, because the recorded response of Peter begins with his affirmation that these Gentiles ought to be immediately baptized. In other words, Peter recognized that Christian conversion normatively includes baptism, however God might orchestrate the temporal arrangements of conversion in particular cases. When this text is read alongside others in Acts, the implication is that conversion includes repentance, faith, and baptism from the human side and forgiveness and the gift of the Spirit from the divine side. All these elements belong together, but not in any sort of mechanical way.[7]

Acts 19:1–7

This is one of the most enigmatic texts in the Bible, and it is impossible to be dogmatic about some of the interpretive issues, but it does say something about the meaning of baptism in Acts. Paul meets in Ephesus a group of about twelve men who are called "disciples," but the sense in which they are disciples is not exactly clear. They were "Christians" in some sense, because Paul treats them as people who ought to be indwelt by the Spirit, but he sensed that something was defective in their professed commitment, leading to his questioning whether they received the Spirit when they

---

7. For a convincing defense of this multi-faceted meaning of conversion in Acts, see Robert H. Stein, "Baptism in Luke-Acts," in *Believer's Baptism*, 52-58.

A Look at the Biblical Texts

believed (19:2). When their answer revealed a general ignorance about the presence of the Spirit, he asked them about the essence of their baptism (19:3). When they described it as the baptism of John, Paul reminded them that the point of John's work was to point to Jesus who came after him, and then Paul completed their initiation into faith by baptizing them "in the name of the Lord Jesus (19:5)." It was at this point of their Christian baptism, in which Paul laid hands on them, that they received the Spirit with the outward manifestation of tongues and prophecy (19:6). There are some unclear aspects of this text, but what seems clear is that Christian baptism is assumed to be the normative context in which the gift of the Spirit is experienced.[8]

Acts 22:16

Paul is here explaining to the Jewish crowd the story of his conversion and call to be an apostle to the Gentiles. Here we find some details to add to the story recounted in Acts 9, in particular some of the words of Ananias to Paul. Having declared some of God's purposes for Paul and having declared him free from his blindness, he instructs him, "Get up, be baptized and wash your sins away, calling on his name." Paul's own experience of conversion includes baptism as an appeal for the forgiveness of his sins, in that baptism is the event in which he called on the Lord for that forgiveness. That is to say, baptism is seen here as a kind of acted prayer, not unlike the baptism of John, in which penitent sinners confessed their sins and sought forgiveness for entrance into the kingdom of God. That should alert us to avoid any thought that Paul drives a wedge between faith and baptism in his epistles, to which we now turn.

---

8. For a full discussion of this text, see Bruner, *A Theology of the Holy Spirit*, 207-214; and Dunn, *Baptism in the Holy Spirit*, 83-89.

Rethinking Baptism

Romans 6:1-4

After Paul develops the doctrine of justification by faith apart from works (Rom 3-5), in order to avoid false inferences about acceptance of a sinful lifestyle, he explains that salvation involves more than justification. As we have already seen in Acts, God gives to us, through faith, not only the forgiveness of sins (dealing with our bad record), but also the gift of his Spirit (dealing with our bad heart). This transformation is described in these verses in terms of a spiritual death and resurrection now, in advance of bodily resurrection yet to come. But when Paul describes the radical transformation that occurs in this life, he links it to our baptism. Conversion is described as inclusive of "baptism into Christ," which is thus a baptism into his death and resurrection. A natural reading of the text indicates that, by baptism "into Christ," we are now "in Christ" with all that this idea entails.

But is union with Christ really achieved by baptism? That says far more than the average Baptist preacher is prepared to say, and although Baptists are happy to use this text as a support for immersion as the mode of baptism, it seems to say far too much about the efficacy of baptism. There is one escape, though, and that is to argue that the baptism in view here is actually the baptism of the Spirit, not baptism in water, and some interpreters take this route of escape.[9] However attractive that option might seem to be, it does not appear to be on target. The language of this text looks like the language of water-baptism, not Spirit-baptism, in the wider NT usage.

The linguistic link between water and Spirit goes back to the words of John the Baptist: "I baptize you in water for repentance, but he will baptize you in the Spirit" (with slight variations in the Gospel accounts). But notice that in the comparison, Christ is to Spirit-baptism what John is to water-baptism, i.e., the baptizer. In Romans 6, Christ is not the baptizer, but instead he is the goal

---

9. For example, Gay, *Baptist Sacramentalism*, 205-215, who takes the same approach in other texts that use baptismal language without explicit reference to water.

of the baptism, the one to whom believers are connected by this baptism. That is not the language of Spirit-baptism. Furthermore, the Romans language of baptism "into Christ" (*eis Christon*) recalls the Matthew 28 language of baptism "into the name" (*eis to onoma*), and that text is clearly talking about water-baptism. The only reason why one might argue that Romans 6 is not talking about water-baptism is the assumption that such realistic language about the efficacy of baptism would be foreign to Paul, but according to Acts 22:16, Paul was very comfortable with such language.

How, then, does this correlate with Paul's insistence that we are justified by faith and not by works? Doesn't this high view of baptism smuggle works into justification? The answer is, of course, resoundingly negative. When Paul talks about works in Romans (and Galatians), what he has in view are works of the Mosaic Law. Paul does not include baptism in the category of works any more than he includes, say, repentance in that category. Baptism is, in fact, something that we allow to be done to us, and in that way it is a fitting way to express faith and grace. For Paul, faith and baptism are like two sides of a coin, distinct but never disconnected, both looking to Christ for the benefits of salvation—the one as attitude and the other as act.

Colossians 2:11–12

This is the one other place in Paul's epistles where he uses the language of burial and resurrection to describe the experience of grace with a connection to baptism. The putting away of the old life is here described via the metaphor of circumcision, which in new covenant salvation is a circumcision "not performed by human hands (2:11)," but this spiritual circumcision is manifested physically through burial "with him in baptism" (2:12). This "resurrection" that we experience after "death" to the old life is explicitly said to be "through faith in the working of God." This last phrase clearly shows that, for Paul, faith and baptism are the inner and outer aspects of one reality. Baptism is the great transition from old life to new because it is the vehicle of faith, not because there is any power inherent in the ritual.

Galatians 3:26–27

Just as Colossians 2 is connected to Romans 6 through the language of burial with Christ, Galatians 3 is also connected to Romans 6 through the language of baptism "into Christ." I have argued above that "baptism into Christ" is naturally read as a reference to water-baptism, and that applies to this text as much as to Romans 6. What is striking about this text is the ease with which Paul moves from faith in Christ in verse 26 to baptism in verse 27 as markers of being "in Christ" and thus "Abraham's seed" (3:28). This epistle is perhaps Paul's strongest affirmation of justification by faith apart from works, and the inclusion of 3:27 in this epistle is one more piece of evidence that, for Paul, baptism and works are in very different categories.

Ephesians 4:5

Paul's exhortation to maintain unity with fellow believers is here grounded in a series of spiritual realities common to all believers, one of which is "one baptism." It looks as if the natural sense of verse 5 is to say that we have one Lord, one common attitude of faith in the Lord, and one formal affirmation of that faith in baptism. In other words, the experience of initiation into union with Christ is also initiation into union with Christ's people, and the shared memory of baptism enhances our sense of connection to one another. One of the foundational identity markers of the body of Christ is baptism into that body.

But some resist this reference to baptism for the same reason that they resist the reference in Romans 6 and Galatians 3—they fear that this attributes an excessive significance to baptism and nullifies the reality of justification by faith alone. I still remember a seminary professor who put it this way: "Ephesians 4:5 a reference

A Look at the Biblical Texts

to water-baptism? Are you kidding? Ephesians 4 is talking about things that unite Christians, and nothing has divided Christians more than water-baptism. This is obviously a reference to Spirit-baptism." The most obvious problem with that kind of reasoning is, of course, the fallacy of reading centuries of baptismal confusion back into a first-century document. One could just as easily argue that Spirit-baptism has been a major source of division in the church, certainly since about 1900, but in any case it is wrong to assume that a doctrine or practice that divides today also divided when Paul wrote Ephesians. A reference to Spirit-baptism in 4:5 would in fact be redundant, because Paul has already asserted the reality of "one body and one Spirit (4:4)," which is essentially the truth of Spirit-baptism.

Does this mean, then, that those who have not been validly baptized should not be considered members of the body of Christ? That would treat baptism as not just normative but absolutely necessary, and that would indeed elevate it to an excessive significance. But seeing water-baptism in Ephesians 4:5 does not imply this. What we have here is one example of the difficulty of drawing a straight line from every New Testament text to our modern context. All of Scripture is relevant for us, but not always in a simple, straight-line way. Paul can write this statement in the way that he does, because at that point in the apostolic church, believers and the baptized were one and the same. Alas, that is not the case today. If Paul were giving the same exhortation today, his words would surely be a bit different.

1 Peter 3:21

This verse is just one of the interpretive challenges in Peter's stream of consciousness here. Does 3:18 indicate that Jesus' resurrection was spiritual and not physical? Does 3:19 say that Jesus preached the gospel and offered salvation to dead people? Does 4:6 say the same thing? But those are for another time. Here we are concerned with the reference to baptism as that which saves us in 3:21. That reference comes about because of Peter's earlier mention of the spirits who were disobedient "in the days of Noah," the days when only Noah's family members were saved "through water," which finds fulfillment in the water of Christian baptism, through which believers in this age of fulfillment are saved.

Clearly Peter is saying that baptism saves in some sense, but in what sense? Ultimately, of course, it is God who saves, and he does so "by the resurrection of Jesus Christ"—any saving efficacy related to baptism is due to its connection to the risen savior. Furthermore, Peter clarifies that it is not the "removal of dirt from the body" (i.e., the physical act itself) that is crucial in the human response. What counts is the inner reality that is expressed in baptism—"the pledge of a good conscience toward God." There is, admittedly, some debate about the exact meaning of the word *eperōtēma*. The KJV translates it "answer," but that is almost certainly not the meaning. Contemporary commentators have defended both "pledge" and "request" as the meaning of the word. The latter may well be the point of the word, given its relation to the verb *eperōtaō* (to ask or request),[10] but in either translation the point of the statement is that the commitment of the inner person is the crucial aspect of baptism. Still, it is true that the physical act of baptism is the means of expressing this commitment. It is here, as in Acts 22:16, an acted prayer that reaches out to the risen Lord for salvation.

Possible allusions to baptism

To this point we have been looking at NT texts that explicitly refer to baptism. I have argued that all of them are talking about water-baptism, although some interpreters have suggested that some of them are referring to Spirit-baptism. Beyond these texts there are some others that refer to water in some way and thus might be allusions to the water ritual of Christian conversion. Given the lack of explicit baptismal terminology, one would not want to build a

---

10. Schreiner, "Baptism in the Epistles," in *Believer's* Baptism, 70-71.

A Look at the Biblical Texts

doctrine of baptism on these texts, but it is worthwhile to ask what they might imply if in fact they do allude to baptism.

John 3:5 gives us Jesus' description of spiritual rebirth as a matter of being "born of water and the Spirit." Given the story of John's baptism that both precedes and follows this episode, an allusion to baptism here would seem to be a very natural reading of the text, but at least two alternatives have been suggested.[11] First, some have argued that birth "of water" is a reference to physical birth, also described as flesh giving birth to flesh in this text (3:6), which means that Jesus is emphasizing the idea of being born "again." This is unlikely, because the grammar of the statement seems to link water and Spirit closely as two aspects of the same birth (in that the two nouns are objects of one preposition). John's way of contrasting the two ideas is "born of *flesh*" versus "born of the *Spirit*." Second, some have suggested that "water" here may be a metaphorical reference to the cleansing and renewing nature of the new birth, with the language coming from prophetic anticipations of God's work in the new covenant (e.g., Ezek 36:25–27).[12] This interpretation may well be true, and if so, there would be no clear allusion to baptism at all, but it is hard to read this text within its wider context and not think of baptism when confronted by the reference to water. In any case, the reference to rebirth in 3:8 as simply "born of the Spirit" is a powerful reminder that John has no intention to magnify the power of baptism. If there is a baptismal allusion here, the point would remain that whatever significance might be attributed to baptism, the ultimate necessity is the work of the Spirit, and baptism is efficacious only as an instrument by which the Spirit makes rebirth a conscious experience.[13]

Titus 3:5 refers to God's saving work as one that is done "through the washing of rebirth and renewal by the Holy Spirit."

---

11. Concise descriptions of the options can be found in many sources, including Carson, *The Gospel According to John*, 191–196; Morgan-Wynne, "References to Baptism in the Fourth Gospel," in *Baptism, the New Testament and the Church*, 121–126; Gross, "The Interpretation of John 3:5," in *Foundations* 62 (Spring 2012).

12. Carson, *John*, 195–196.

13. As argued by Gross, "John 3:5."

The Greek *loutron* (bath, washing) would be an apt way to refer to baptism, and earlier Baptist writers often assumed that baptism is in view.[14] The issues here are essentially the same as in John 3:5, and the same conclusions seem to be warranted. There may be a reference here to baptism as a means that God graciously uses to mediate the experience of spiritual renewal, but if so, baptism has value only as an instrument of the Spirit who is the powerful actor in spiritual rebirth.[15]

Ephesians 5:25–26 uses the term *loutron* as in Titus 3.5 and connects it to the "word" (Greek *rhēma*), and this "washing with water through the word" is a means that Christ uses to purify his church-bride. The emphasis of the passage is on the self-sacrificial love of Christ for the church, his giving up of himself to make the church holy, and it is difficult to see how the event of baptism is a sacrificial act of Christ. However, it is also difficult to see what "washing of water through the word" might denote as an aspect of Christ's sacrifice. It is probably easier to see an allusion to baptism as the event in which the word of the gospel is proclaimed, and a word of confession is spoken by the baptizand, and that event as one step in Christ's work of making the church all that it needs to be. There may, then, be an allusion here to baptism as one step in the process of sanctification. It would be difficult to say more based on this text.[16]

Hebrews 10:22 refers to the Christian experience of "having our bodies washed with pure water." This serves as the final reason for assurance to draw near to God, following references to the blood of Jesus, the removal of the curtain of the old covenant, the high priestly ministry of Jesus, and the inner experience of a clear

---

14. For example, Keach, *Baptism Refin'd; or Baptism in its Primitive Purity*, 82–83. Keach was one of the most influential Baptist leaders of the 17th century and one of the primary authors of the Second London Confession of 1689, thus a representative of mainstream Baptist thought, not an eccentric.

15. This is the view of Schreiner, "Baptism in the Epistles," 85, and this is further evidence that Schreiner and I are defending essentially the same doctrine of baptism, even though he refuses to use the term "sacramental" to describe it.

16. Ibid., 84.

conscience (10:19–22). Given that "bodies" here are set over against "hearts", and that washing of the body is a descriptor of Christian experience, it is hard to deny that we have here an allusion to baptism. The point seems to be that the inner experience of forgiveness and the outward experience of baptism are the subjective and objective seals of access to God through Christ. In a Christian context, what could washing of the body refer to if not baptism?

Summary

When thinking about the relation between salvation and baptism, one fundamental question is this: Do we get baptized because we are sinners seeking Christ, or because we are disciples bearing witness to a previously completed conversion? Most Baptists (at least in North America) today would give the second answer, but the baptism texts of the New Testament seem to point toward the first answer. As I have argued above, the baptism texts point toward union with Christ, the forgiveness of sins, and the gift of the Spirit as benefits received through baptism. The one exception to this is Acts 10 and the conversion of Cornelius's Gentile household, when the Spirit is poured out prior to baptism. But even there, Peter calls for immediate baptism, pointing to salvation without baptism as an anomaly. Furthermore, the Spirit is given in that episode prior to any expression of faith ("as they were listening"), but we do not infer from that fact that salvation occurs apart from faith.

But there are many other texts that speak of salvation through repentance and/or faith with no reference to baptism at all. How do we correlate that with a high view of baptismal efficacy? There are several things that need to be said, but one is to note that several of the baptism texts themselves make the point that what is crucial is the faith expressed in the event. Beyond that, we need to note that Paul's emphatic statement of *sola fide* in Romans and Galatians is directed at a Jewish misuse of Mosaic Law, not an overemphasis on baptism. In fact, in those very epistles he refers to our having been baptized into Christ. The writers of the New Testament do not separate faith and baptism, and neither should we.

There is one other baptism text that demands attention, because on the surface it appears to diminish the significance of baptism in a way that makes it hard to say all that I have said above. The text is 1 Corinthians 1:13–17, especially Paul's distinction between baptism and preaching the gospel.[17] What shall we make of this? This is part of Paul's response to the Corinthians having created factions based on their attachment to particular Christian teachers (Paul, Apollos, Cephas, Christ[!]). In order to emphasize the unique and central role of Christ over his servants, Paul asks the rhetorical question, "Were you baptized in the name of Paul?" Now, why ask that question? The answer is likely that some were creating factions based on which preacher of the gospel baptized them, but that is in effect to recognize the great significance of baptism. If baptism were an afterthought, then who would create factions based on that? Paul then expresses his gratefulness for the fact that he baptized so few of the Corinthians, so that they would not be tempted to attach themselves too closely to him. For the most part, he preached and left the baptizing to his colleagues. All this is both a reminder that the gospel is the heart of the matter, and that baptism is sufficiently crucial as a response to the gospel to serve as a basis for misguided idolization of the baptizer.

So here is where the evidence goes, as I see it: God has provided baptism to mediate saving union with Christ at the level of conscious experience. It is not that we cannot be saved without baptism, but it is that baptism is the normative way in which faith comes to tangible expression, and salvation becomes an assured reality. Can we be saved without baptism? Of course we can—God's grace is not limited by our failure to do everything right. But that is not the right question. The right question is, how does God intend baptism to function? And the answer of the biblical text is that God intends it to serve as a defining moment of conversion, the way in which the penitent sinner *formally* says yes to the gospel and receives the salvation offered by God through Christ.

---

17. Gay considers this text to be the "clinching passage" in his attempt to refute a sacramental view of baptism. See Gay, *Baptist Sacramentalism*, 245-260.

A Look at the Biblical Texts

Think of it this way: Evangelical Christians recognize that when a person comes to believe in Christ and the gospel, that person needs to do something to seal and confirm that reality. The most common thing that we do is to offer to lead the person in a prayer expressing that attitude of faith. But do we lead them to thank God for salvation already experienced? No, we lead them to ask Christ for salvation, even though the prayer presupposes that faith is already present. Think of baptism, then, as an acted prayer that God has commanded (remember Acts 22:16 and 1 Pet 3:21). It is also common for preachers of the gospel to ask people to respond by doing something like walking to the front of the room (an altar call), using language like, "Come forward to be saved." Does that mean that the preacher believes that there can be no salvation apart from walking the aisle? Of course not, but simply that walking down the aisle is one way to translate belief into action and respond to Christ as an embodied person. Now, what if the response called for is to be baptized? That sounds very much like the New Testament.

Chapter 3

Questions and Answers

IF YOU HAVE READ this far, you probably have questions (perhaps many!) about the implications of this redefinition of the meaning of baptism for the practice of evangelism, church membership, the relation of baptism to the Lord's Supper, assurance of salvation, or even the definition of the gospel. I understand that, and although I am sure that what follows is not comprehensive, this is my honest attempt to respond to legitimate questions. In my experience, these are the most common (and understandable) concerns.

Does this view of baptism deny that we are saved by grace alone through faith alone?

This is a very understandable question, given the way that North American evangelicals usually think about salvation, but this is a misunderstanding at various points. The view that I am defending here understands baptism as conversion-baptism or faith-baptism, i.e., an expression of repentance and faith that has value only as such an expression. There is no value in the act of baptism as such, no ritual magic invoked in the event. Furthermore, salvation is not a reward for the act of baptism; acceptance of baptism is simply the formal way to receive the gift of salvation.

Questions and Answers

A sacramental understanding of conversion-baptism would deny the Pauline teaching about justification by faith alone only if baptism were a "work" in Paul's mind, but that is a misreading of the apostle's concerns. When Paul affirms justification by faith in Romans and Galatians, he is setting faith in Christ against adherence to Mosaic Law, thus arguing that Jews and Gentiles are accepted by God in the same way. His essential point is about Christ versus Torah, not faith versus baptism. When Paul says "faith alone," is he saying "by faith, not by repentance?" Of course not, as he makes clear in a text like Acts 26:20. Conversion can be denoted by either repentance or faith, or by both together, each assuming the other. Similarly, Paul assumes that baptism accompanies faith, as is evident in Galatians 3, where those who are saved can by described either as those who have faith in Christ (3:26) or as those who have been baptized into Christ (3:27). Baptism is a "work" only in the sense that it is something that we do, but the same thing could be said of faith. Believing the gospel is something that we must do to be saved, even though it is not a physical act. The mere fact that we do it does not make it a "work" in Paul's terms.

Justification by grace alone through faith alone in Christ alone is language rooted in the Protestant Reformation of the 16th century, but the major reformers in both the Lutheran and Calvinistic streams all thought of baptism in sacramental terms. The Lutheran tradition has always spoken of baptism as a means of regeneration, while emphatically affirming justification by faith alone, which means that it is historically inaccurate to see a sacramental view of baptism as opposed to the understanding of the gospel recovered in the Reformation. I think it is accurate to say that the baptismal theology that I have proposed is essentially a Reformed/Calvinistic view as applied to confessing believers. The Reformed tradition refers to baptism as a "sign and seal" of inclusion in the covenant people, and the crucial word is "seal." I would not argue that the term "seal" is ever used in Scripture to refer directly to baptism, but at a conceptual level it seems to capture the biblical balance in which faith is the crucial reality on the human side of salvation, but baptism ratifies faith experientially. As a seal, baptism ratifies both God's offer of grace and the human reception by faith, as Calvin argues:

> It seems to me that a simple and proper definition would be to say that it is an outward sign by which the Lord seals on our consciences the promises of his good will toward us in order to sustain the weakness of our faith; and we in turn attest our piety toward him in the presence of the Lord and of his angels and before men. Here is another briefer definition: one may call it a testimony of divine grace toward us, confirmed by an outward sign, with mutual attestation of our piety toward him.[1]

Even though I am not convinced by Calvin's application of this to infants (who have no faith to ratify), it makes very good sense of the biblical linkage between the benefits of salvation and baptism for confessing believers. To say "sacrament" is to say "grace," not to introduce a means of gaining merit before God. Even in the Catholic tradition that does speak of merit earned during the Christian life, baptism is not conceived of as a means of gaining such merit. In Catholic thought, baptism conveys sanctifying grace that empowers obedience, but it is obedience in the form of acts of love for God and others that leads to merit. However baptism may be described, it is not in biblical terms a meritorious "work."

Does this make baptism necessary for salvation?

If, as I have argued, the Bible indicates that we get baptized to experience salvation, then one might infer that salvation does not come apart from baptism. That would lead to all sorts of concern about family members and friends who profess to be Christians but have never been baptized as a believer. Clearly this question is very relevant, because it determines how we relate to everyone around us. But I think we can relax a bit and recognize that a high view of baptism does not imply that the grace of God is bound

---

1. Calvin, *Institutes of the Christian Religion*, Book IV, Chap. XIV, 1.

to baptism in such a way that our failure to use baptism properly nullifies saving grace.

Can we be saved without being baptized? Of course we can. Luke makes that clear in Acts as he tells the story of Cornelius and his household, in that God poured out the Holy Spirit upon them prior to any response on their part. But to ask if we can be saved apart from baptism is really to ask the wrong question. The right question is, how does God intend baptism to function? Or, what blessings does God intend to bestow via baptism? There is little value in asking which divine provisions are optional and which are required—if God has ordained them, then they are for our benefit, and that should be our focus.

When is a person actually saved, at the point of faith or at the point of baptism?

The answer to this question is that a person is saved when God declares the person righteous and bestows his Spirit to indwell the person, but only God knows exactly when that is. This question actually assumes a separation between faith and baptism that appears to be foreign to the New Testament witness. We know only the outward evidence of God's saving work, and we therefore must treat people according to the evidence. In fact, when we talk about the "point of faith," we are really talking about the "point of initial evidence of faith." When someone verbally confesses faith and gives no reason to doubt that confession, then we treat the person as a saved believer, but we also tell the person to confess faith in baptism. "Salvation" in New Testament terms is not just a momentary thing. There is a sense in which we have been saved (Eph 2:8–9), and a sense in which salvation is a future experience at the return of Christ (Rom 13:11), and apparently a sense in which we are being saved progressively (1 Cor 1:18). The point is that salvation is a comprehensive reality, and it is not all experienced at one point in time. As an experiential reality, salvation comes at the first awareness of faith, is confirmed in baptism, is enhanced as spiritual growth occurs, and will be completed in the age to come.

Our task is not to discern the exact moment of justification, but to call people to every step along the path of salvation.

Is it wrong to delay baptism until a church service or until a class on baptism?

If I read the New Testament accurately, baptism is described there as conversion-baptism, the way in which a repentant sinner says yes to the gospel and formally becomes a Christian. If so, then coming to faith and baptism need to be connected as closely as possible, but we need to think through this question carefully. We don't live in the apostolic age, and we can't always draw a straight line from then to now. Furthermore, the Bible does not give as much guidance as we might like to answer this question. There is no New Testament example of a baptism occurring during a church meeting, but we actually have very little description of church meetings of any sort. The closest we come is 1 Corinthians 14, and it is more about correcting abuses than about detailing what ought to be done. There is no direct biblical statement about who ought to serve as the baptizer, and Baptists have never been unanimous on that point. When biblical texts tell us that certain people were baptized, there is usually no explicit statement as to the exact amount of time between verbal confession and baptism, although the texts seem to give the impression that the Pentecostal pattern of baptism on the same day was normal.

The heart of the matter seems to be that the baptizand must give a credible confession of repentance and faith, and must also understand that baptism is the divinely ordained way to formalize that confession of faith. The time required to bring about that understanding will vary, no doubt, from one person to another. An immediate dip in the swimming pool may be appropriate for some, but it is hard to see why a delay until the following Sunday would be problematic. A class of some sort to clarify baptism may facilitate an intelligent experience of baptism, but the point of the class is to clarify conversion and baptism, not to deal with the details of the church doctrinal statement.

Questions and Answers

I can't see in the Bible any distinction between joining the universal church and joining the local church, but at our stage in history the universal church is fractured in ways not envisioned in the Bible. This, I think, may justify separating baptism from local church membership, thus allowing for the time to explain the nature of the particular local church and facilitate membership with integrity. To put it another way, baptism should be closely connected to conversion and entrance into the universal church, while thoughtful entrance into membership in the local church may require post-conversion instruction.

What about calling people to immediate baptism in response to the preaching of the gospel? This might be done when baptisms are already planned for the end of the service, and the invitation to be baptized is extended after a sermon that communicates the gospel and the meaning of baptism as a personal response to the gospel, or the invitation could stand on its own. I can't see any reason to reject such a practice, and it certainly seems to fit with the biblical picture. The most common objection, I suppose, would be the concern that this might stimulate an impulsive response on the part of some who are not truly converted and thus give them a false assurance. Clearly this could happen, but the same thing could happen in connection with any kind of response to the proclamation of the gospel. The assumption underlying this objection is often that we are responsible to make sure that John or Jane is saved before we baptize them, but this assumption must be challenged. I know that such inspection of conversion narratives is common in Baptist history, but it is hard to see the biblical evidence for it. If that approach had been followed in Samaria by Philip (Acts 8), then Simon the Sorcerer would never have been baptized, but in fact he was baptized. We are not failures if some whom we baptize later fall away from the Lord, any more than our Lord himself was a failure when some of his disciples turned away. The parable of the sower (Matt 13; Luke 8) told us right at the beginning that some would have a temporary kind of faith. Faith is confessed in baptism, but the genuineness of faith is tested after baptism.

What difference would this make in our practice of evangelism?

If evangelism is defined narrowly as the communication of the good news itself, i.e., the news of what God has done in Jesus Messiah to bring salvation and the kingdom of God (especially through Jesus' death and resurrection), then nothing is affected. But if evangelism is defined as inclusive of our communication of the response demanded by the gospel, then we are forced to consider some changes to our common practice. In my evangelical Baptist tradition, the response called for is essentially a prayer confessing one's need, affirming one's belief in Christ's atoning death (and perhaps his resurrection), and asking God for salvation through Christ. In a private setting, there is probably no physical act apart from the prayer, but in a public setting the prayer may be connected to going forward at an "altar call" or going to speak to someone after the conclusion of the meeting. This focus on a prayer-response is perfectly appropriate, because prayer is always appropriate as we relate to God, but what follows may require some rethinking.

In my circles, those who evangelize are often told to give the responder immediate assurance of salvation, and perhaps of eternal security, thus indicating that conversion is a completed reality. Perhaps what is lacking is an immediate suggestion that this newly expressed faith needs to be sealed in the way that God designed, i.e., in baptism. Depending on the knowledge of the new believer, this may call for an agreement to be baptized at the earliest possible time, or it may call for an agreement to receive instruction about baptism and its significance. In either case, we can emphasize the power of symbols to translate mental commitment into experience, perhaps sharing our own experience of baptism.

Questions and Answers

If baptism is designed to be conversion-baptism, does it make sense to baptize people who have been disciples for a long time but have never been baptized as a believer?

I think the answer is yes, but it is a legitimate question. The people in view may have been baptized as infants and later affirmed their personal faith by living as disciples of Christ, or they may have become disciples without any experience of baptism for various reasons. Given the disjunction between conversion and baptism that is common in Baptist practice, some people become believers in such a context and just never get around to baptism, since it is "only a symbol" anyway. I have to admit that baptism for such people does not have exactly the same significance that it has in the biblical baptism narratives, because they are not becoming disciples in the act. Nevertheless, baptism in these cases can still have a sealing or confirming function, and my pastoral experience has shown me that baptism at any stage of life can be a powerful means of grace. Baptism is more than an act of obedience, but it is at least that, and delayed obedience still has spiritual benefits. As a pastor I have baptized many people in this category, and I have observed something powerful happening in their baptism. It is not about power in the water, but it is about a divine-human encounter that occurs when faith in Christ is expressed in such a powerful symbol. If God provided it, then it is no surprise when he does something powerful in the event to confirm our connection to him.

If a church is committed to immersion as the mode of baptism, should rebaptism by immersion be required for people who were baptized as believers by other modes?

I have often heard Baptists say something like, "We don't baptize infants—we believe in baptism by immersion." I know what they mean, but the comment actually treats two issues (the subject of baptism and the mode of baptism) as if they were one, a confusion typically rooted in lack of understanding of the diversity of the universal church. In Eastern Orthodoxy, infants are baptized, but normally by triple immersion; but in most Anabaptist traditions, baptism is usually by sprinkling or pouring, although it is for believers only. In Roman Catholic and paedobaptist Protestant (Anglican, Lutheran, Reformed, Methodist) traditions, adult converts who have never been baptized are baptized as confessing believers, but in most cases not by immersion. In other words, some people experience conversion-baptism by modes other than immersion, and some of them want to become members of Baptist (or other immersionist) churches. This creates a dilemma for such churches, and I know this well from my experience as a pastor and elder in Baptist churches.

One can make a cogent case for both positive and negative answers to this question. *On the rebaptism side:* Baptism is supposed to be done by immersion, and it is always possible to get it right, whatever may have been done before. The confessional baptism done by another mode may well have been a significant personal experience, but it wasn't baptism in the biblical sense. Furthermore, the integrity of church membership demands it. Members of immersionist churches must be immersed if they really believe what the church believes. *On the non-rebaptism side:* It seems clear that immersion is the best mode of baptism, but to say that it is absolutely necessary for validity may be an overstatement. And assuming that non-immersion is an anomaly, it seems that a second confessional baptism disconnected from conversion and initiation into discipleship is a greater anomaly. While it may get the mode right, it seems to get the function wrong, making baptism more about connection to a particular kind of church than it is about connection to Christ.

I have vacillated on this debate over the years, but I have become increasingly convinced that we should not ask for rebaptism in these cases. To a great extent, this is an implication of my conviction that baptism is intended to be the sacramental seal of conversion—a once and for all ratification of faith and discipleship that stands at the dawn of Christian experience. For that reason, it does seem to me that a second confessional baptism simply does not function in the way that baptism is designed to function. I will admit that my thinking is shaped by my experience of trying to explain to a potential church member that their confessional baptism is not considered valid by my church, due to the inappropriate way in which water was applied, and the awkwardness and lack of conviction that I felt. But the disappointment expressed by the applicant for membership and my tentativeness may be, I think, rooted in a biblical theology of baptism as a defining moment in conversion. Given that significance, it is appropriate that we would lack the desire to repeat it just to get the mode right.

Another part of my reasoning relates to the case for immersion as the mode of baptism. There are, I think, basically four arguments for immersion: (1) The basic meaning of the verb (*baptizō*) and nouns (*baptismos*, *baptisma*) that describe baptism is dipping or immersion, as everyone admits. (2) The biblical narratives of baptism seem to assume or demand a dipping action. (3) Only immersion adequately symbolizes the radical change that baptism signifies, a change so radical that it can be called death and resurrection (Rom 6; Col 2). (4) Every Christian tradition (Catholic, Orthodox, Protestant) recognizes immersion as valid baptism, but that is not true for other modes, so Christian unity is served by immersion.

This reasoning does, I think, lead us to the practice of immersion as the norm, but as a case for the absolute necessity of immersion, there are some possible weaknesses: (1) Although all authorities agree that dipping is the basic meaning of the baptism word-group, there seem to be some exceptions to the rule. For example, in Luke 11:38, the action expected of Jesus before a meal is described using *baptizō*, but the ritual is likely the hand washing that is described elsewhere (Mark 7:1-4). That is to say, the person is said to be "baptized" if the hands alone are dipped and washed. In Hebrews 9:10, the writer uses the plural of *baptismos* to describe ritual washings of the Old Covenant, and the washings described in the context (vss. 13, 19, 21) are sprinkling rituals. It would be useful to say that "baptize" simply means "immerse," but that would be to oversimplify the conclusion. (2) None of the narratives describe the action of baptism per se, although some do refer to "going into" and "coming out of" the water (e.g., Acts 8:38-39) to describe movement to and from the river or pool. Baptizing in a body of water like the Jordan River could be done by standing in the water and pouring water over the head. We know that baptisms occurred in the river, and there are good reasons to conclude that it was by full immersion (otherwise, why go into the river?), but the action is not described explicitly. (3) It does seem that the action of immersion underlies Paul's comments in Romans 6 and Colossians 2, but we need to recognize that Paul does not say in so many words that baptism *pictures* burial and resurrection. What he says is that baptism unites us to Christ, and thus to his death, burial, and resurrection. Immersion best pictures this transformation, but that is not quite equivalent to saying that only immersion is a valid mode. (4) The argument from Christian unity cuts both ways. Yes, doing baptism by immersion is affirmed by all traditions, so doing it that way will eliminate some tensions. But the oldest traditions (e.g., the *Didache*, dating from perhaps the start of the second century) affirm diverse modes even if immersion is preferred, and in the absence of any biblical texts that explicitly address the question of mode as an issue, Christian unity might call for acceptance of diverse modes.

In the end, given the fact that there is some inference involved in making the case for immersion as the necessary mode, and given the fact that a second confessional baptism does not function in the way that God designed baptism to function, I suggest that Baptist and other immersionist churches ought not require rebaptism of persons who were baptized previously by other modes.

Does this view of baptism imply close communion?

"Close communion" (sometimes phrased "closed" or "strict" communion) denotes the view that limits participation in the Lord's Supper to those who have been validly baptized, and in a Baptist context, that means that only those who have been baptized as believers by immersion are invited to the Table. Those who hold this view do not deny the salvation of other believers who have not been properly baptized, but they argue that the order expressed in Matthew 28:19-20 and the nature of Communion as a church ordinance call for this restriction. Close communion was the dominant Baptist view until the twentieth century, but Baptists have never been unanimous on the question. The Second London Confession (1677/1689) was for two centuries the most influential confession among Calvinistic Baptists, and in an appendix to the confession, the signatories admit their difference of opinion and the consequent lack of comment on the issue in the confession. In the twentieth century, most Baptists moved in the direction of "open communion" in which all who confess faith in Christ are invited to the Table. I understand and respect the arguments in support of close communion, but ultimately I find them unconvincing.[2]

I have no doubt at all that in the apostolic age, the invitation to Communion was for those who had been baptized as believers, but this is because in the primitive church, the believers and the baptized were the same people. Baptism was the way that sinners formally became believers without delay, and it was assumed that one of the commonalities of believers was their "one baptism" (Eph 4:5). But that is simply not true today. If we exclude from Communion those whom we recognize as brothers and sisters in the family of God, then we are saying that even though they clearly believe what is signified and proclaimed in Communion, and they thus are rightly regarded as sharing in the benefits of Christ's atoning work, they are still not permitted to declare that with us Baptists. That strikes me as incoherent at best, and willful division of the body of Christ at worst. The Lord's Supper is a proclamation of the gospel, not a proclamation of ecclesiological distinctives.

But are paedobaptists excluded from Communion because they are disobedient disciples? This has been asserted by many Baptists over the years, on the grounds that baptism is the first

---

2. For contemporary perspectives both pro and con on the matter of close communion, see two chapters in Schreiner and Crawford, eds., *The Lord's Supper: Remembering and Proclaiming Christ Until He Comes*. In support of close communion see Gregory A. Wills, "Sounds from Baptist History," and in support of open communion see Ray Van Neste, "The Lord's Supper in the Context of the Local Church."

act of obedience, and the application to paedobaptists is obvious. Should those believers be baptized as believers? Yes, I think so. But are they disobedient disciples? No, unless they admit that they ought to be rebaptized but refuse to do so. We are talking here about people who sincerely believe that the children of a believing parent ought to be baptized, and they are obeying Christ as they understand his teaching. If we agree to share Communion only with those who are in full agreement with us about the demands of Christian discipleship, then we may not need many chairs for our Communion service.

Will this sacramental view of baptism cause people to trust in baptism rather than trust in Christ?

Paul seems to refer to this sort of thing in 1 Corinthians 10:1–5. It appears that some of the Corinthians assumed that their participation in baptism and the Lord's Supper guaranteed their salvation, but Paul vigorously attacks this falsehood. There is always the temptation to trust in the means of grace rather than God who bestows grace, but this is not limited to baptism. For example, there are many people who think that they are securely saved because they prayed the right prayer, and they can give the time and place when they did so, but this is flatly denied by our Lord in Matthew 7:21–23. It is God who saves—neither faith nor baptism is a savior. God is the savior, and faith and baptism are instruments by which God makes salvation real in our experience (cf. Mark 16:16). This is not to say that faith and baptism relate to salvation in precisely the same way—faith is absolutely necessary, and baptism is only relatively necessary—but it is to say that verbal profession of faith is no more a guarantee than is baptismal profession of faith.

Ultimately all we can do is teach the truth about the gospel, salvation, and baptism faithfully, seeking to clarify at every opportunity. We are not responsible for the ways in which our listeners may distort the teaching. Is it possible to make too much of baptism? Of course it is. But avoiding overstatement is no justification for understatement.

Questions and Answers

Is this view of baptism the first step toward paedobaptism?

Some paedobaptists[3] and some credobaptists[4] have argued that a sacramental view of baptism logically leads to the practice of infant baptism. The basic argument is something like this: If we understand baptism as a means of grace, and if God's grace is prior to our response, then it is reasonable to baptize infants as a sign of God's grace. Restricting baptism to confessing believers assumes human response prior to grace, and this reverses the order in salvation. If baptism is a divine act of grace, then the human act is not a necessary component.

The short answer to the question is this: No, this does not logically lead to paedobaptism. To say that baptism is a sacramental means of grace is not to say exactly how it mediates grace. What I have argued is that baptism is designed by God to be a meeting place of grace and faith. As such, baptism mediates union with Christ at the level of conscious experience. Baptism is a sacrament of experienced salvation, not a sacrament merely of the promise of salvation to come later through faith (as in infant baptism). Baptism is about initiation into discipleship, not about deliverance from the womb and initiation into the church nursery.[5]

How can this view be called Baptist, since Baptists have always considered baptism to be a symbolic ordinance, not a sacrament?

There are at least two aspects to this answer. *First*, one of the fundamental principles of Baptists (and other Protestants) is the unique and final authority of Scripture. This means that all of our interpretations of Scripture and our confessional statements are subject to reformation by further study of Scripture. Even if Baptists have

---

3. For example, Flemington, *The New Testament Doctrine of Baptism*, 137; Cullmann, *Baptism in the New Testament*, 50–51.

4. For example, Gay, *Baptist Sacramentalism*, 106-118.

5. I have argued this at length in *More Than a Symbol*, 211-219.

never said it this way before, it still might be right, and Baptists might need to change. *Second*, in spite of the common rhetoric, it is not true that Baptists have always been anti-sacramental. In fact, the baptismal doctrine that I have tried to articulate here has deep roots in the early (seventeenth century) Baptist literature, and even though it faded into the background for some time, it was recovered by British Baptists in the twentieth century.[6]

First, a point about terminology. Many Baptists are fond of saying that one Baptist distinctive is a belief in "two ordinances, baptism, and the Lord's Supper." However, in early Baptist literature, the category of "ordinance" is inclusive of things other than baptism and the Lord's Supper. For example, the seventeenth-century *Baptist Catechism* says this:

> Q.93. What are the outward Means whereby Christ communicates to us the benefits of Redemption?
>
> A. The outward and ordinary Means whereby Christ communicates to us the benefits of redemption, are his Ordinances, especially the Word, Baptism, the Lord's Supper, and Prayer: all which Means are made effectual to the Elect, through faith, for Salvation.[7]

There are four ordinances listed here, but the word "especially" suggests that there may be more, and in some Baptist confessions the category also includes a post-baptismal laying on of hands for a special work of the Spirit.[8] The contents of the category, then, are somewhat fluid. The catechetical statement also speaks of the ordinances as means by which Christ applies his saving work to individuals, which indicates that "ordinance" does not imply "non-sacramental."

Baptism and the Lord's Supper are, indeed, recognized as ordinances with a special kind of connection to the gospel, and thus

---

6. I have provided extensive evidence for this claim in *More Than A Symbol*, 10-155.

7. Ibid., 18.

8. Among General Baptists, *The Standard Confession* (1660), and among Calvinistic Baptists, *The Philadelphia Confession of Faith* (1742).

these two alone are called "sacraments." For example, the Orthodox Creed of 1678 says, "Those two sacraments, viz. Baptism, and the Lord's-supper, are ordinances of positive, sovereign, and holy institution."[9] This shift of terms from "sacrament" to "ordinance" occurs frequently in early Baptist literature, indicating that the contemporary Baptist nuancing of the terms is an innovation, not a continuation of the Baptist tradition.

Out of all the evidence in early Baptist authors, I will give here just two examples of their high view of baptism. The first example is from Thomas Grantham, the leading theologian of the General (Arminian) Baptists:

> Baptism in the ordinary way of God's communicating the grace of the Gospel is antecedent to the reception thereof, & is propounded as a means wherein not only the Remission of our sins shall be granted to us, but as a condition whereupon we shall receive the gift of the Holy Ghost . . . [It] was fore-ordained to signifie and sacramentally to confer the grace of the pardon of sin, and the inward washing of the Conscience by Faith in the Bloud of Jesus Christ.[10]

The second example is from Benjamin Keach, one of the leading theologians of the Particular (Calvinistic) Baptists:

> Consider the great Promises made to those who are obedient to it, amongst other things, Lo, I am with you always, even to the end of the World. And again, He that believeth, and is baptized, shall be saved. If a Prince shall offer a Rebel his Life in doing two things, would he neglect one of them, and say this I will do, but the other is a trivial thing, I'll not do that? Surely no, he would not run the hazard of his Life so foolishly. . . . "And then in Acts 2.38. Repent, and be baptized every one of you for Remission of Sin, and ye shall receive the Gift of the Holy Spirit: See what great Promises are made to Believers in Baptism.[11]

9. Fowler, *More Than a Symbol*, 19.
10. Ibid., 28.
11. Ibid., 29.

When these comments are read in the context of the larger books from which the quotes are taken, it is obvious that neither Grantham nor Keach believed that there was any kind of power in the act of baptism itself, or that there is no possibility of salvation apart from baptism. But they did clearly believe that baptism is the act of a repentant sinner responding to the gospel, not the act of an already confirmed disciple of Christ. There are many factors that have created this divergence of modern Baptist thought from the early Baptist tradition, but whatever those factors may be, we ought to admit that there is nothing unbaptistic about a sacramental understanding of believer baptism.

What does this view of baptism imply about the age at which we baptize children who profess faith?

This is probably the greatest challenge faced by all credobaptists: how do we relate this conversionist theology of baptism to children who grow up with Christian nurture in the family and the church from day one? The baptisms described in the New Testament are consistently conversion baptisms, i.e., the baptism of Jews who come to believe that Jesus is Messiah or of Gentiles who turn from idols to serve the true God and Jesus Messiah, but the baptism of children born to believing parents is not exactly like that. Such children are not repenting of false religious commitments, but they are instead affirming their commitment to the gospel that they have heard all along the way.

It is easy to see how one can argue this in two different ways. On the one hand, one might argue that baptism is about initiation into discipleship, and if the sacrament is to embody a serious commitment to follow Christ as an obedient disciple, then it may be appropriate to delay it until one is old enough to make independent decisions about long-term commitments. That would delay baptism until later adolescence or perhaps even early adulthood. On the other hand, one might argue that baptism is one's initial confession of faith, the first step in learning what it means to follow Christ, and Jesus clearly recognized a genuine faith in children, even a paradigmatic kind of faith to be imitated by adults (Matt 18:1–6). If childhood faith is genuine, and baptism is designed to be the outward expression of that, then baptism of pre-adolescent children may be defensible.

I confess that I have vacillated on this question for a long time, because I can feel the force of the argument in either direction. Gradually, however, I have found my thought gravitating toward the practice of earlier baptism, given the significance of baptism as an initiating sacrament rather than the culmination of a prolonged journey with Christ. It is hard to choose a minimum age, because children are so diverse in their experience of faith. What seems reasonable to me is to baptize such children only if it seems clear that they are requesting it apart from any external pressure, and only if they are old enough for it to be a memorable experience. There are legitimate concerns about this practice, to be sure, but what are we saying to children who are part of the life of the church when we refuse to mark their confession of faith via baptism? In my circles, it is not uncommon for parents to allow their children who have confessed faith to share in the Lord's Supper, while at the same time delaying their baptism, but what would justify admission to the one without the other? I think that parents allow their children to participate in the Lord's Supper because of their recognition of evident faith that they want to nurture, but a credible confession of faith is equally a basis for baptism in New Testament terms.

But how can we really be sure about confession of faith by such children? Aren't they just doing what they know will please their parents? Aren't we setting them up for confusion when they enter adolescence and may begin to question what they have been taught? Isn't there a high probability that they will wander away from faith and (hopefully) return, and then as adults doubt the validity of their baptism? Those are fair questions that I have asked myself, but I'm not convinced that they destroy the case for childhood baptism. After all, we can never be absolutely sure about anyone's confession of faith, and if we accept the New Testament evidence for baptism as inherent in conversion, then it is always true that the test of genuineness comes after baptism, not before it. And why would we doubt that nurture by Christian parents is a normal pathway to genuine repentance and faith? I recognize that if we delay baptism until adolescence, then we are positioning it at a point where children begin to act more independently, but I am not sure that delaying baptism until those often tumultuous years solves any problems. In fact, peer pressure is typically more intense at that age, and the possibility of baptism due to external pressure may actually be greater. Perhaps it would be better to remind adolescents of their prior experience of baptism as an encouragement to obedience.

I understand the complexities of this question, and I suggest that we credobaptists ought to admit that it creates difficulties as we try to apply our theology of baptism. I confess that it is enough to make me take a fresh look at the case for baptizing the infant children of believing parents, which would eliminate this particular difficulty. But although I have taken a fresh look at the case for paedobaptism (in fact, several times), I am still convinced that the point of baptism is to be a meeting place for grace and faith, and I am thus still a convinced credobaptist. However, we ought to be honest enough to admit that applying our theology is not always simple, and we really ought to devote some time to discussion of this question about the appropriate age for baptism.

If I was baptized as a professing believer, but I am convinced now that my true conversion actually occurred much later, should I be rebaptized as a seal of my conversion?

Historically, Baptist theologians have argued that believer baptism should not be repeated, but in recent history in some Baptist circles, it has become common for individuals like these to be rebaptized (occasionally multiple times). It appears to me that the historic view is probably correct on this point, so that I would oppose a second believer baptism in almost all cases. A biblical text that bears on this point is Romans 6, where Baptists generally recognize that Paul draws a parallel between the Christ-event and the baptism-into-Christ-event. Just as the work of Christ involved death-burial-resurrection, so also baptismal union with Christ involves the burial of the old self and the resurrection of a new self, a spiritual coming to life that foreshadows the bodily resurrection yet to come. In that context, Paul also emphasizes that the death of Christ was once and for all (vs. 10), and that finds an echo in the decisive transformation inherent in Christian conversion. For that reason, it seems that Christian baptism should also be a once and for all event.

I would personally accept the idea of a second believer baptism in a case in which the individual knows that the first baptism was a conscious charade, with no intent at all to confess faith in Christ, but few of the cases that we are talking about are of that character. The more typical case is one in which the person was baptized prior to adulthood, experienced some struggles spiritually, wandered off the path of discipleship for some time, then experienced a spiritual crisis that brought the person back to the Lord. Looking back on all of this, one might wonder if they were really regenerate at the time of baptism, and this is a perfectly understandable question. But to what extent is the question answerable? How much ability do we have to assess what was in our experience several years or even decades ago? We recognize that the journey of the Christian life is not a straight line onward and upward, and we may experience various crises along the way. Ultimately God alone knows who is truly regenerate, and baptism is only an identification of the apparently regenerate. If we wander off the path of discipleship, the proper response is repentance that gets back on the path, not starting all over again.

If converts are baptized without an ongoing demonstration of their faith, will this work against regenerate church membership and responsible congregational governance?

Baptists are fond of saying that they (we) are committed to regenerate church membership, indeed, that this may be the most important Baptist distinctive. Baptists have also tended to support congregational church governance, but if important spiritual decisions are going to be made by the membership as a whole, then it is clearly important to ensure that members are actually regenerate believers. The result, then, is that Baptist churches have often demanded an articulate conversion narrative with a post-conversion chapter and perhaps some awareness of church doctrine prior to admitting a candidate to baptism.

Let's start with the terminology. I understand what is being said in the affirmation of "regenerate church membership," but it may not be the best way to say it. What we are really affirming is that church members must be people who credibly affirm that Jesus is Lord, people who give evidence of personal commitment to Christ, and not just evidence of a Christian heritage in their family. In other words, the church is a community of *apparently* regenerate persons. We all admit that there may well be unregenerate persons within the church membership, some of whom may have given powerful outward evidence of belonging to Christ (Matt 7:21–23; Heb 6:4–6). So the idea that we can know with certainty that the members of the church are all regenerate is simply wishful thinking. We ought to take church discipline seriously, much more seriously than we commonly do, and that is the means by which the church membership is limited to those who claim to be born again disciples. I doubt that I can overturn the traditional use of the phrase "regenerate church membership," and it is hard to come up with a simple alternative, but I am arguing that we should understand the limits of what we mean when we use the phrase.

With regard to governance, there are several things to be said. We all recognize that in all but the tiniest of congregations, many of the decisions are made by appointed leaders and not by congregational vote, and given the biblical indications that elders/overseers do in some sense rule (1 Tim 5:17) and are to be obeyed (Heb 13:7, 17), it may be appropriate to tilt the decision making process further in the direction of the appointed leaders. That would be one way to avoid having significant decisions made by immature believers or by unregenerate persons. Another possible approach would be to require a period of post-baptismal discipleship prior to admission to voting membership. Given the fractured nature of the universal church in our day, and thus the diverse polity among churches, it might be wise to require some intelligent commitment to the local church's distinctives prior to voting privileges as a part of congregational governance. We ought to admit that we have very little biblical evidence of the exact way in which churches in the apostolic age made decisions. The evidence of Acts 15 with regard to doctrinal parameters (the debate about requiring circumcision and submission to the Law of Moses for Gentile converts) shows a special authority of the apostles and elders. If the governing role of church members is largely to affirm biblically grounded decisions proposed by the elders (as in Acts 15), then the immaturity of those recently baptized need not be a major problem. If, on the other hand, the church decides to create a gap between baptism and voting membership, that seems to be less of a problem than creating a gap between conversion and baptism. Baptism is about union with Christ, not union with a particular kind of church.

If baptism occurs this quickly as an element of conversion, what does this imply about the testimony given by the candidate at baptism?

Evangelicals are fond of testimonies, stories about our experience of God in our lives, and for good reason, because the Christian life is about experience and not just doctrine. The apostle Paul can speak in a very matter of fact way about, for example, the experience of the Holy Spirit in the believer's life (Rom 5:5; 8:16). However, I am not convinced that baptism is ordinarily the time to expect such a testimony, although I admit that I am a bit of a reformer on this point. In my local church, we ask baptizands to give a testimony of their conversion experience to the whole congregation (in our case via a pre-recorded video played while they stand in the baptistery), and some of them are quite moving and encouraging. But they are often moving because they describe a long-term Christian experience, with some ups and downs, and baptism is described as an act of obedience to which God has finally brought them. I am grateful that they are confessing their faith in this way finally, but such testimonies bear little resemblance to the baptism narratives of the Bible. The Philippian jailor, for example, had little story to tell when he and his household were baptized in the middle of the night, the same night in which he asked how to be saved.

In biblical terms, the person receiving baptism needs only to credibly express repentance for sin and faith in Jesus Christ. It would seem, then, that answering questions about those matters is the only kind of testimony that is required for baptism. The Bible does not give us a formula for this, so I assume that the questions can be phrased in various ways. If we have baptizands give lengthy testimonies, this may be very encouraging to baptized believers who are present, but it also may create a barrier for others. Some who are present may have been attending church and hearing the gospel for some time, and they know that they now believe the gospel, but they have very little story to tell, and they just can't see themselves doing what they have observed. A special group is children who have grown up in the nurture of their family and church. They may not remember a time when they did not believe, and they have no history of a rebellious lifestyle for which they need to repent. Their testimony is basically, "I have been nurtured from the beginning to believe in God and to trust in Jesus for the forgiveness of my sins and the power to follow him, and I want to confirm that I believe that." I remember when my youngest son was being baptized at age sixteen, and he struggled to write a testimony because there was little before-and-after to tell, and I know that he is not alone. There is a place for encouraging one another by talking of God's ongoing work in our lives, but the baptistery may not be the best place.

Questions and Answers

If I agree that baptism is in some sense sacramental and an inherent part of becoming a Christian, how do I teach this as a pastor in a church that has traditionally rejected that idea?

The short answer is, "with all patience and instruction" (2 Tim 4:2). Having done this in two churches without precipitating a split, I think I can say a bit about how this might work out. The first thing to recognize, I think, is that terminology is not the issue. You do not need to force the term "sacrament" on anyone, given the fact that neither "sacrament" nor "ordinance" is a biblical term describing this category. That fact, in itself, is one thing you need to teach. The question then becomes, how does the Bible describe baptism in relation to conversion and union with Christ? Your role as a pastor-teacher demands, then, that you help the people in your church look at the actual biblical references to baptism and seek to synthesize what is there. In my experience, it is easy to convince people that the biblical texts on baptism seem to attribute to baptism a significance greater than what has been typically been taught in Baptist churches. As one of my seminary professors was fond of saying, it is amazing what we learn when we actually look at the text.

In the process of teaching the biblical material relating to baptism, it is important to emphasize what is *not* being taught. In other words, emphasize that this is not about some kind of magical power inherent in baptism; that this is not saying that baptism conveys anything mechanically apart from being an expression of repentance and faith; and that this is not saying that apart from baptism there can be no salvation. People don't always hear it the first time, so you will have to say it more than once, and in various ways. With some of this teaching in place, you can invite people to baptism when you invite them to faith, and when you baptize new believers, you can describe it as a defining moment in conversion. I leave the details to you.

Chapter 4

Conclusion

WHAT I HAVE PROPOSED in this small book is what might be called a Reformed Baptist sacramental understanding of the meaning of Christian baptism. I recognize that it presents a model that differs in significant ways from the typical view of baptism held by my fellow Baptists and other credobaptists, but I believe that it has solid roots in the earliest Baptist thought and, more importantly, in the baptismal texts of the New Testament. My appeal is that we attempt to formulate a baptismal theology that arises naturally from the explicit and implicit references to baptism in the New Testament, and I believe that when we do that, we end up with the view that baptism is inherent in Christian conversion. In biblical terms, we become Christians by baptism, because baptism is the divinely ordained way in which we confess repentance and faith in Jesus Christ, the formal way in which we say yes to the gospel and accept salvation from the Lord. At least, that is the way that God plans for it to happen. As I have argued in this book, this is what would be called a sacramental view of baptism, but the terminology is not the issue. The issue is to accept baptism in all its biblical fullness, which involves moving beyond the idea of baptism as merely a backward-looking symbol of an already completed conversion. Such a view reduces baptism to sheer obedience, often just the final condition of formal church membership, disconnecting it

Conclusion

from conversion and destroying the mystery of faith's response to the offer of grace. Whatever terminology you may use, I hope you will join me in an attempt to reintegrate baptism into the experience of conversion. It is a dramatic ritual suitable for the dramatic transformation that occurs when grace meets faith.

This is a small book on a multi-faceted topic, and you may want to explore this in greater depth. If so, here are some suggestions for helpful sources. I might as well begin by shamelessly recommending my own book, *More Than a Symbol*, which develops the argument of this small book in much greater detail. That book will also give you a glimpse of Baptist thought about the sacramental question by looking at the writings of key figures in British Baptist life over the four-hundred years of Baptist history. The evangelical sacramentalism that was present in early Baptist literature in a relatively undeveloped form was reformulated in much greater depth by British Baptists in the twentieth century, starting with H. Wheeler Robinson at the beginning of the century and culminating with the work of G. R. Beasley-Murray in the 1960s. The most convincing and influential work in that reformulation is Beasley-Murray's *Baptism in the New Testament*, a book that is recognized as a classic by theologians of all traditions. As a combination of biblical exegesis and theological synthesis, it is virtually without peer.

Anthony Cross surveyed both the theology and practice of baptism among British Baptists in *Baptism and the Baptists*, and this book covers the subject in great detail. After Cross's book and mine were published in Paternoster's series, "Studies in Baptist History and Thought," there was a renewed interest among Baptist scholars in the study of baptism in particular, and sacramental theology more generally. This led to the publication in that series of *Baptist Sacramentalism*, edited by Anthony Cross and Philip Thompson. I contributed a chapter in that book on reactions to the book *Christian Baptism*, a 1959 publication that created a bit of a public furor with its defense of a high view of baptismal efficacy. A sequel, *Baptist Sacramentalism 2* (not the most elegant or creative of titles) was published in 2008, also edited by Cross and Thompson. My contribution to that book was a chapter on "Baptists and Churches of Christ in Search of a Common Theology of Baptism." Both of the edited volumes include authors from both North America and Great Britain, thus demonstrating that the fresh thinking that originated in Great Britain in the twentieth century had begun to find an echo on this side of the Atlantic. The chapters in both volumes look at a range of issues concerning baptism and the Lord's Supper, but also explore other themes like ordination and sacred space.

In 2006, Thomas Schreiner and Shawn Wright edited an outstanding collection of essays entitled *Believer's Baptism: Sign of the New Covenant in Christ*, written mostly by Southern Baptists. Although the authors are wary of sacramental language (as the editors make clear in their reference to my book), several of the chapters articulate an understanding of baptism that is, as I see it, essentially equivalent to what I have argued in this book. I am thinking especially of chapters by Robert Stein, Thomas Schreiner, Jonathan Rainbow, and Ardel Caneday.

The fresh thinking on baptism represented by the books I have listed above caught the attention of a young PhD student at Calvin Theological Seminary named Brandon Jones. Brandon and I had a long conversation about this as a potential dissertation topic at the meeting of the Evangelical Theological Society in 2008, and I served as the external examiner for his dissertation in 2011. His work was published in revised form the next year, entitled *Waters of Promise: Finding Meaning in Believer Baptism*. He is generally supportive of this reformulation, but he argues for a stronger focus on covenant theology as a way of describing the goal of baptism.

The most extended and elaborate articulation of this "high" view of conversion-baptism is now Anthony Cross's *Recovering the Evangelical Sacrament: Baptisma Semper Reformandum*. Cross has been at work on this topic as both author and editor for about twenty years, and this is the fruit of his labors. It could do for this generation what Beasley-Murray's book did for his.

Conclusion

And finally, there are at least a couple of books from outside the Baptist fold that Baptists ought to read and discuss. John Mark Hicks and Greg Taylor wrote *Down in the River to Pray: Revisioning Baptism as God's Transforming Work*. Hicks and Taylor write within the Stone-Campbell tradition, in their case the a cappella Churches of Christ part of that tradition. This book is biblical, theological, historical, and practical, and it is a stimulating attempt to situate baptism in all those contexts. As the sub-title indicates, it is in various ways a revisionist contribution to the Churches of Christ tradition, and as such, it is an example of what I have described elsewhere as a convergence of the Stone-Campbell and Baptist traditions. More recently, Hicks wrote *Enter the Water, Come to the Table*, which extends his insights to the Lord's Supper as well. As I see it, this convergence of which I speak is in fact developing among scholars in both traditions, with members of both groups recognizing that our traditional conceptions of baptism require some fine-tuning. I do not know the extent to which that scholarly convergence has filtered down to the pulpit or the pew, but I certainly hope that it does. That, after all, is why I wrote this book.

Bibliography

Beasley-Murray, G. R. *Baptism in the New Testament*. Grand Rapids: Eerdmans, 1962.

Bruner, Frederick Dale. *A Theology of the Holy Spirit*. Grand Rapids: Eerdmans, 1970.

Calvin, John. *Institutes of the Christian Religion*. Ed. John T. McNeill. Trans. Ford Lewis Battles. Philadelphia: Westminster, 1960.

Carson, D. A. *The Gospel According to John*. Grand Rapids: Eerdmans, 1991.

Cross, Anthony R. *Baptism and the Baptists*. Studies in Baptist History and Thought, Vol. 3. Carlisle, UK: Paternoster, 2000.

———. *Recovering the Evangelical Sacrament: Baptisma Semper Reformandum*. Eugene, OR: Pickwick, 2012.

———, and Philip E. Thompson, eds. *Baptist Sacramentalism*. Studies in Baptist History and Thought, Vol. 5. Carlisle, UK: Paternoster, 2003.

———. *Baptist Sacramentalism 2*. Studies in Baptist History and Thought, Vol. 25. Carlisle, UK: Paternoster, 2008.

Cullmann, Oscar. *Baptism in the New Testament*. Trans. J. K. S. Reid. London: SCM Press, 1950.

Dunn, James D. G. *Baptism in the Holy Spirit*. London: SCM Press, 1970.

Flemington, W. F. *The New Testament Doctrine of Baptism*. London: S.P.C.K., 1953.

Fowler, Stanley K. "Baptists and Churches of Christ in Search of a Common Theology of Baptism." In *Baptist Sacramentalism 2*, ed. Anthony R. Cross and Philip E. Thompson. Studies in Baptist History and Thought, Vol. 25. Carlisle, UK: Paternoster, 2008.

———. "Is 'Baptist Sacramentalism' an Oxymoron?: Reactions in Britain to *Christian Baptism* (1959)." In *Baptist Sacramentalism*, ed. Anthony R. Cross and Philip E. Thompson. Studies in Baptist History and Thought, Vol. 5. Carlisle, UK: Paternoster, 2003.

———. *More Than a Symbol: The British Baptist Recovery of Baptismal Sacramentalism*. Studies in Baptist History and Thought, Vol. 2. Carlisle, UK: Paternoster, 2002.

Bibliography

Gay, David H. J. *Baptist Sacramentalism: A Warning to Baptists*. Biggleswade, UK: Brachus, 2011.

Gill, John. *A Body of Doctrinal and Practical Divinity*. Paris, AK: The Baptist Standard Bearer, 1989; orig. published 1769-1770.

Gross, Oliver. "The Interpretation of John 3:5." *Foundations* 62 (Spring 2012).

Hicks, John Mark. *Enter the Water, Come to the Table*. Abilene, TX: Abilene Christian University Press, 2014.

———, and Greg Taylor. *Down in the River to Pray: Revisioning Baptism as God's Transforming Work*. Siloam Springs, AR: Leafwood, 2004.

Jones, Brandon G. *Waters of Promise: Finding Meaning in Believer Baptism*. Eugene, OR: Pickwick, 2012.

Keach, Benjamin. *Baptism Refin'd; or Baptism in its Primitive Purity*. London: Nathaniel Crouch, 1689.

Mantey, J. R. "The Causal Use of *eis* in the New Testament." *Journal of Biblical Literature* 70 (1951): 45-48.

Mounce, William H. *Basics of Biblical Greek*, second edition. Grand Rapids, MI: Zondervan, 2003.

Porter, Stanley E. and Anthony R. Cross, eds. *Baptism, the New Testament and the Church*. Sheffield, UK: Sheffield Academic Press, 1999.

Robertson, A. T. *Word Pictures in the New Testament*, 6 vols. Nashville, TN: Broadman, 1930-1933.

Schreiner, Thomas R. and Matthew R. Crawford, eds. *The Lord's Supper: Remembering and Proclaiming Christ Until He Comes*. Nashville: B&H Academic, 2010.

——— and Shawn D. Wright, eds. *Believer's Baptism: Sign of the New Covenant in Christ*. Nashville: B&H Academic, 2006.

Turner, Nigel and James Hope Moulton. *A Grammar of New Testament Greek*. 3 vols. Edinburgh: T. & T. Clark, 1963.

www.ingramcontent.com/pod-product-compliance
Lightning Source LLC
Chambersburg PA
CBHW051708090426
42736CB00013B/2591